What Is God's Design for My Body?

What Is God's Design for My Body?

Susan Horner

Moody Publishers
CHICAGO

©2004 by
SUSAN HORNER

All rights reserved. No part of this book may be reproduced in any form without permission in writing from the publisher, except in the case of brief quotations embodied in critical articles or reviews.

All Scripture quotations, unless otherwise indicated, are taken from the *Holy Bible: New International Version®*. NIV®. Copyright © 1973, 1978, 1984 by International Bible Society. Used by permission of Zondervan Publishing House. All rights reserved.

Scripture quotations marked NKJV are taken from the *New King James Version*. Copyright © 1982, 1992 by Thomas Nelson, Inc. Used by permission. All rights reserved.

Scripture quotations marked NCV are from the *Holy Bible, New Century Version*, copyright © 1987, 1988, 1991 by Word Publishing, Nashville, TN 37214. Used by permission.

Book Interior Design by *www.designbyjulia.com*
Some images / photos © Ablestock.com, PhotoDisc, Arttoday.com, and Photos.com

ISBN: 1-8024-0923-7

1 3 5 7 9 10 8 6 4 2

Printed in the United States of America

Dear Parents,

What Is God's Design for My Body? is the third and final book in the Miracle of Creation series. The purpose of this book is to edify and build up your teens and preteens through role models and noble truths. I have tried to write a nonembarrassing, discreet series that paints a picture of godly sexuality.

This book was not written to answer every question your child may have. It is a foundation for you to build upon, a springboard for more conversations with your child. The book was written in three sections, so don't feel that you and your child need to read it all in one sitting. The truths are timeless, so you can ask your children to reread it when they are older to reinforce and remind them that "there is a time for everything, and a season for every activity under heaven" (Ecclesiastes 3:1).

Sincerely,
Susan Horner

 OUR LIVES ARE ALSO MADE OF TIMES AND SEASONS!

God's Design For Our Bodies

If you have ever taken a jump on a dirt bike, done a flip turn in a swim meet, or baked a cake, you know that "timing is everything." The seasons we experience as our planet whirls around the sun show us that our brilliant Creator is a God of timing.

Our lives are also made of times and seasons. These seasons are not the literal winter, spring, summer, and fall, but they are stages, experiences, or milestones in life. Your family has celebrated each season of your life: when you took your first steps, dressed yourself in mismatched clothes, tied your own shoes, wiggled your baby teeth loose, and finally balanced yourself and took off on a two-wheeler bike.

THE CHANGES WILL NOT HAPPEN OVERNIGHT

Now you're about to enter a new season. This season is when a boy matures into a man and a girl blossoms into a woman. Each boy and girl's body develops in its own time. The changes will not all happen overnight; they are more like the transformation of a caterpillar into a butterfly.

The Creator God, who designed you, also wants to be your loving heavenly Father. He wants to help you be successful in this new season of your life, especially when you feel self-conscious or awkward. As the butterfly opens its wings to the sun to dry and then takes to the sky, so you too can grow into an awesome man or woman, who takes responsibility for your choices and enjoys the freedom that comes with maturity.

Soon chemical messengers called hormones will act like an alarm clock ringing in your bloodstream.

SUSAN HORNER

The amazing organs that make it possible for you to someday become a father or mother will wake up and develop. Here are some of the changes you can expect.

About Young Men

The hormonal alarm clock will ring inside a boy's body sometime between ages twelve and fifteen. Boys have two testicles between their legs. Each one is made of tightly rolled tubes and is in the shape of a ball. Each awakened testicle starts to manufacture more testosterone.

Testosterone is the hormone that causes boys' voices to go deeper, their muscles to get stronger, and their faces to grow beards.

READ PROVERBS 5:16–18 TONIGHT!

Inside each testicle life-giving sperm are made, as many as a million a day. The two testicles hang in a sac called the scrotum behind a boy's penis. When a young man's testicles start making sperm, the sperm builds up and eventually needs to be released from the body. A common time for sperm to be released is during sleep. This is normal and to be expected. Just as more blood flows into arm muscles when weights are being lifted, more blood will flow into the penis, causing it to stiffen and swell before it releases sperm. The sperm will flow from the testicles through a tube called the Ductus Vas Deferens. Then the sperm will mix in the prostate with a watery fluid called *semen*.

SUSAN HORNER

GOD WANTS YOU TO KEEP YOUR MIND AND BODY PURE.

The semen and sperm empty into another tube, called the urethra. The fluid then flows through the urethra and out the penis opening.

Proverbs 5:16–18 compares a man's body, mind, and soul to pure, life-giving streams of water—valuable water that should not be spilled on the streets to run wherever it wants to go.

Proverbs 20:29 conveys that part of being a young man is feeling proud of, or glorying in, your physical strength. In 1 John 2:14 the apostle John wrote,

"I wrote to you, young men, because you are strong, and the word of God lives in you, and you have overcome the evil one."

WHAT IS GOD'S DESIGN FOR MY BODY?

PAUL QUINER DOWNER IS A COLLEGE JUNIOR MAJORING IN BIBLICAL STUDIES AND BUSINESS ADMINISTRATION.

Guys, movies, TV shows, and video games are telling us lies about what it is to be a real man. They tell us that masculinity is about blowing things up, doing whatever we want to, manipulating others, and looking out for number one. Over the years I have learned:

- A real man honors God, others, and the gift of his own life and body—even when it's tough.

- A real man knows that anyone can mindlessly do what feels good, but it takes strength of soul to stand firm in the face of temptation.

SUSAN HORNER

You will find yourselves growing stronger as you grow into men.

- A real man is grateful for his parents as teammates whom God has given him to help him achieve God's best for his life.

- A real man is a protector who earns trust by guarding others rather than selfishly using them.

- A real man is committed to making choices he will not have to hide or regret.

- A real man strives not only for outward purity but also for inward purity.

- And finally, a real man knows that the most masculine thing in the world is a man who seeks to know God and loves His Word.

A SECRET GARDEN SURROUNDED BY HIGH WALLS

About Young Women

Girls, your body is like a beautiful garden. The private places of your body deserve to be protected. In fact, God's Word compares your body to a secret garden surrounded by high walls, with a locked gate to keep trespassers away (Song of Songs 4:12). As your body awakens and matures, you will feel a need for even more privacy when you bathe and dress.

God designed and formed a woman's body in a wonderful way.

A woman's body is perfectly designed to protect and nurture a baby as it grows inside her womb. As a girl's body begins to mature, her breasts will develop as the mammary glands prepare to someday nurse a baby.

Girls and women have one almond-shaped *ovary* on each side of their pear-shaped uterus, or womb. Connected to each side of the womb is a hollow fallopian tube. When a girl's body begins to mature, one of the ovaries will release an egg about once every twenty-eight days. The egg will be caught up and swept into one of her fallopian tubes.

During the first twenty-four hours that the egg is in the wide outer part of the fallopian tube, it rolls slowly along, waiting to be fertilized by a male sperm. The egg will then journey five or six

days through the slender part of the tube as it makes its way to the womb. At the end of the egg's journey through the tube, it lands inside the womb.

If a male sperm does not fuse with the egg when it first enters the fallopian tube, the egg crumbles and leaves the woman's body when the womb cleanses itself. Just as deciduous trees shed their leaves in the fall, so the womb sheds and cleanses itself of its lining because the lining is not needed.

When the blood-rich lining is released from the womb, it flows out of the womb through the vaginal canal, which is also called the vagina.

The womb then starts preparing again for the next egg that will be released. This twenty-eight-day cycle of preparing and cleansing is called a woman's menstrual cycle. When the womb sheds its lining, we say a woman is having her period or is menstruating.

SUSAN HORNER

NOW IS AN IMPORTANT TIME IN YOUR LIFE TO ASK HIM FOR WISDOM

As you grow into a woman, let your heart grow soft and your spiritual ears be attentive to the One who loves you with an everlasting love. If you have given your heart to Jesus, then you are a princess of the King of kings. He longs to crown you with wisdom and escort you to the high places of good choices. Now is an important time in your life to ask Him for wisdom and study His Word.

GOD CREATED MAN IN HIS OWN IMAGE; IN THE IMAGE OF GOD HE CREATED HIM . . .

God's Design for Marriage and Families

The beauty of the seasons and the magic of perfect timing also applies to marriage and families. The book of Genesis tells us on the sixth day of creation God made all the different land animals. Then "God created man in His own image; in the image of God He created him; male and female He created them" (Genesis 1:27 NKJV). First God formed a man out of the ground and named him Adam, which comes from the root word

for earth or dirt in the Hebrew language. Adam was a lifeless clay man until God breathed His own breath into Adam's nostrils, and the man became a living being.

Could it be that children get a kick out of making mud pies and most people enjoy sculpting sand castles because we inherited the desire to get our fingers in the sand and mud from our Creator whose image we bear?

SUSAN HORNER

MARRIAGE WAS GOD'S GIFT TO ADAM AND EVE.

God brought every animal and bird He had formed to Adam to name. Adam had the animals to enjoy, clear pools of water to swim in, and God to talk to in the cool of the day, yet God said, "It is not good that man should be alone; I will make him a helper comparable to him" (Genesis 2:18 NKJV).

So the Lord God caused the man to fall into a deep sleep. As Adam slept the Lord took one of Adam's ribs and then closed up the skin. With the rib God made a woman, and then He brought her to the man.

Adam was very excited and pleased that God had made someone especially for him. At this very first wedding God blessed them and said, "A man will leave his father and mother and be united to his wife, and they will become one [body]" (Genesis 2:24).

Adam and Eve walked naked through the garden, and they

WHAT IS GOD'S DESIGN FOR MY BODY?

were not ashamed. And God saw all He had created and said, "It is very good."

Marriage was God's gift to Adam and Eve, and it is still precious and holy to Him. God intended marriage to be like protective walls around a loving home—a home where children could feel safe and loved by both their mother and father.

A biblical wedding is between a man and a woman who have chosen to forsake all others. The bride and groom face each other and promise to love,

SUSAN HORNER

honor, and care for each other: in both the happy and sad times; when there is plenty of money and when there does not seem to be enough; when they are healthy and when they are sick. **They promise to be there for each other even when they don't feel like it.**

The bride and groom give each other rings to remind themselves and all other people that their promise is until one of them dies. Jesus said, "So they are no longer two, but one. Therefore what God has joined together, let man not separate" (Mark 10:8–9).

Those are some big promises! How can anyone keep such promises, and for so many years? We all have friends who have hurt our feelings, or whom we like one day but feel annoyed with the next. How can a husband and wife love each for their whole life?

HE HAS MADE EVERYTHING BEAUTIFUL IN ITS TIME!

God intended the wedding covenant to be a promise between a man, a woman, and Himself, like three strands of fiber twisted into one strong rope. Both the husband and the wife need to ask God to help them to keep liking, loving, and caring about the other person's feelings. Read 1 Corinthians 13:4–7 to see what every marriage needs to grow.

After the bride and groom are pronounced husband and wife, their new life together, their new adventure, as a married couple begins. Ecclesiastes 3:11 says, "He has made everything beautiful in its time" (NKJV). Now the pure and perfect time has come for the bride and groom to consummate, or complete, their marriage promise. Just as when Adam and Eve were first naked and did not feel ashamed, the bride and groom do not need to feel embarrassed to be naked with each other. For now they are husband and wife and have God's blessing upon their becoming one body.

SUSAN HORNER

It is not just about seeing each other without their clothes but being naked with their hearts—they don't have to cover up what they are hoping and dreaming about. They can be who they really are and not be afraid that their spouse will reject them but will love, accept, and know them more deeply than anyone else.

Now is the time for the husband to rejoice in his bride and for the bride to welcome him into the private garden of her body. The husband and wife embrace as they express the love and attraction that they have for each other. Song of Songs paints a picture of a bride and groom consummating their marriage.

The husband rejoices in his bride and says, "You are a garden locked up . . . my bride . . . a sealed fountain."

The bride then welcomes her husband into her private garden by saying, "Let my lover come into his garden. . . ."

SUSAN HORNER

The groom enters and says, "I have come into my garden, . . . my bride."

The husband and wife become one, just as God had planned when He said, "A man will leave his father and mother and be united to his wife, and they will become one [body]" (Genesis 2:24).

The husband comes into his bride's garden, and they become one when his penis enters his wife's vagina.

This oneness between a man and a woman in our language today is called *intercourse*. In the old English language, the word <u>intercourse</u> was used to mean getting to know someone deeply by sharing feelings and ideas through talking. In the Hebrew language when it describes Adam coming inside Eve, it says Adam

knew his wife. And after he knew her she conceived —she became pregnant.

During intercourse a stream of sperm will flow from the husband's testicles, through his penis, and into his wife's vagina, or vaginal canal. The wife will not become pregnant every time she has intercourse with her husband. There are only a few days a month when an egg is in the outer part of the fallopian tube waiting to receive the male sperm.

But when an egg and a sperm do unite, a baby begins to grow. Now instead of cleansing itself, the womb protects and nurtures the rapidly changing fertilized egg called an embryo. The baby's umbilical cord becomes its lifeline to receive food and oxygen.

The baby in the womb can hear someone say, "I love you, little unborn baby." He can also hear people arguing and shouting, and his little body stiffens in fear.

Every baby needs kind and mature parents who will love and care for him before and after he is born. God saw you and loved you with an everlasting love while you were growing in your mother's womb.

When the baby is ready to be born, the mother's body goes

into labor. Labor is rhythmic muscle movements, very much like the waves upon the sea. The womb's muscles squeeze and push the baby through the vaginal canal, also called the birth canal. The vaginal opening enlarges to allow the baby to come into the bright sunlit world.

The baby now takes in nourishment with his mouth and breathes on his own

SUSAN HORNER

using his nose and lungs. The doctor will tie the umbilical cord and cut it. Soon it will dry up and fall off, and the baby gets a belly button.

The newborn baby nurses at his mother's breast, and receives a nourishing, healthy meal. He is happy and content to be close to his mother.

I LOVE YOU, LITTLE UNBORN BABY!

People are able to choose their actions.

God's Design for Our Choices

We can see how imaginative God is by the animals He created. But God chose to create people in His own image, giving us more responsibility and honor than the animals.

Animals do whatever feels natural, but babies grow into young adults like you who are able to make complex, long-term choices. Your choices can have good or bad effects on yourself, other people, animals, and even the earth.

Adam and his wife, Eve, had a wonderful life in their garden paradise. They had lots of freedom and a variety of foods to eat. God only asked them not to eat fruit from one tree. Instead of resisting their tempter, they listened to him and ate fruit from the tree of the knowledge of good and evil. Suddenly, for the very first time, Adam and Eve felt embarrassed that they were naked. They quickly sewed fig leaves together and covered themselves. When they heard God walking in the garden, Adam and Eve ran and hid behind trees.

God was not embarrassed to see Adam and Eve naked. He is the one who designed their bodies. Psalm 139 says we are wonderfully made.

Adam and Eve chose to disobey God. And their choice had consequences. God covered them with an animal's skin and then banished them from their garden paradise.

SUSAN HORNER

THOUGHTS LEAD TO CHOICES.

The animal who was sacrificed to cover Adam's and Eve's bodies was like a picture of how Jesus would come someday as the sacrificial Lamb to cover and forgive our sins.

To read the whole story, turn in your Bible to Genesis, chapters 1–3.

Now our minds are filled with the knowledge of good and evil. And the days of walking naked through the neighborhood with only pure thoughts ended after Adam and Eve disobeyed God.

WHAT IS GOD'S DESIGN FOR MY BODY?

Our minds have become a battleground. And the struggle is with our thoughts, because thoughts lead to choices.

That is why we are told in Philippians 4:8 to think about the things that are true, noble, right, pure, lovely, and admirable.

It's a good idea to think and pray before you let friends talk you into doing things with your body that you will later feel embarrassed about. If you read and memorize God's Word, you will be changed within by a new way of thinking. Then you will be able to decide what

SUSAN HORNER

God wants for you (Romans 12:2). And when you pray, His peace will direct you.

It's true you may feel left out or misunderstood if you choose not to do what everyone else is doing. At these lonely times, ask Jesus to introduce you to other valiant and courageous young men and women who are trying to live by God's standards.

There are young men today who are like noble knights that defend what is good and wrestle against their own temptations.

Paul Downer is one of those men. Listen to what Paul has to say.

"Girls, I know that it is very tempting for you to dress in a way that attracts the attention of guys. But the attention you get by dressing in a

sensual, revealing way is not the harmless attention it might seem to be. It is in fact simple lust. Please, take it from me that this is not the kind of attention you want, and the run-of-the-mill guys you could attract in this way are not the sort you dream of marrying one day. You are worth so much more than that! God has something better in store for you. **So treasure your beauty and honor us men by dressing in a modest, appropriately attractive way."**

SUSAN HORNER

Song of Songs 3:5 (NCV) says,

"Promise not to wake love. Do not excite my feelings of love until I am ready."

Imagine it is winter and you are skiing in the high mountains. All around you and under your feet, seeds are resting and waiting beneath blankets of snow. When spring returns, warm breezes will melt the snow and awaken the seeds. Soon the mountain meadows will look like an artist dipped his brush in colors and swept it across the high places.

Even though your maturing body may feel very much alive

and awake, it is best for you to be like sleeping seeds under blankets of snow, waiting for the right season—until you are safely in a marriage covenant.

Being out of season with our bodies can cause a lot of heartache. A young woman who becomes pregnant before she is married can feel like a bird alone in winter without a nest for her young. Every baby needs a father's love, acceptance, training, and financial support.

Having intercourse before or outside of marriage can cause sickness and diseases. Just as colds and the flu are spread by germs, sexual diseases are passed from person to person. Many of these diseases have no cure. Some cause cancer, others cause painful blisters, and many young people have even died from them. If both the husband and wife wait for each other until they are married, they don't have to worry about these diseases.

Read Genesis 39 to see how Joseph handled sexual temptation. When Potiphar's wife saw how attractive Joseph was, she tried to tempt him, saying, "Lie with me."

Joseph answered, "How can I do this great evil and sin against God?" Day after day she continued to tempt him. Then one day, when all the other servants were

> The biblical Hebrew words often translated as "go into," "know," or "knew" describe a husband and wife in covenant relationship having intercourse. But the Hebrew word used in the Bible to describe people experiencing intercourse outside of marriage is translated "lay with" or "lie with." That is where the slang words "get laid" or "sleep with" come from.

NOW IS THE TIME TO HONOR YOURSELF AND YOUR FUTURE WITH EVERYTHING YOU DO!

gone, she grabbed Joseph by his garment and said, "Lie with me." But Joseph left his garment in her hand and fled outside.

First Corinthians 6:18–19 says, "Flee from sexual immorality. All other sins a man [person] commits are outside his body, but he who sins sexually sins against his own body." Our sensitive minds, souls, and physical bodies can be affected by sexual sin in the same way that pure water becomes contaminated and muddy when it runs into the street. The effect is like a delicate garden after it has been trespassed and trampled upon.

SUSAN HORNER

If someone is trying to pollute, invade or trespass upon you by doing wrong things to your body, know that God never wanted the person to do that to you. Now is the time to tell the person to stop and to ask people you trust to help you. The story at the end of this book is written for you.

Young men, do not try to climb the walls and trespass into private gardens that don't belong to you. Your body and the sperm that comes from you is intended to be shared with only one woman, your wife. "Should your springs overflow in the streets, your streams of water in the public square? Let them be yours alone, never to be shared with strangers. May your fountain be blessed, and may you rejoice in the wife of your youth" (Proverbs 5:16–18).

Aaron St. Jacques will tell you it is worth the wait.

Aaron St. Jacques is a college graduate who enjoys taking walks and stargazing with his wife, Christine.

Imagine that God has set you down in the middle of the biggest candy store you have ever seen. You are surrounded by chocolates, lollipops, jelly beans, gummy bears, and suckers. God says, "If you wait until tomorrow, I will give you all the candy in this store. You may eat all you want, and you won't get sick." Would you believe God and wait eagerly for the next

Susan Horner

Think about helping your mind, personality and spirit grow!

day, or would you snatch a few pieces of candy right away?

Sex is like that candy store. God promised that if we wait until the season of marriage, then we will enjoy pleasures beyond our wildest dreams. When I was eleven, I decided to believe God and trust His timing. Now He has blessed me with a beautiful wife who also chose to wait for me when she was eleven. Christine and I are so happy enjoying the rewards of staying pure.

Girls, only the man who has the privilege of being your husband should enter your garden. By keeping your garden secret and locked you are valuing yourself, and you will be living the way God says is best for you and your future children.

LORI TRANI TELLS HER STORY.

LORI TRANI AND HER HUSBAND, PAUL, LEAD A BIBLE STUDY FOR COUPLES AND ARE LOOKING FORWARD TO RAISING CHILDREN TOGETHER.

I grew up with a "fairytale" view of meeting a handsome, godly, intelligent, romantic, kind prince, falling in love with him, and getting married.

I was told that princes only appeared in fairy tales, and no real guy like that existed. At twenty-five I still had not met a "prince" and was beginning to think I would never marry because my standards were too high. Then Paul walked into my life. He didn't come riding on a white horse, nor did he rescue me from some peril, but he changed my life forever.

SUSAN HORNER

Paul and I had a wonderful attraction to each other, and the sexual temptations became even stronger after we were engaged. Even though I knew that God wanted us to wait until we were married, sometimes I found myself thinking, <u>Since he is going to be my future husband, does it really matter if we are physically intimate now?</u>

I knew it did matter. So I moved out of my apartment and went back home with my mom until our wedding. This offered great accountability for Paul and me.

Our wedding day really was like a fairy-tale. I felt proud to wear white. We had stayed pure and knew God was pleased. Paul had waited for his princess, and I, for my prince. And yes, with God as the focus in our lives, we've been able to live happily ever after.

ANNE WHITE

ANNE WHITE IS STUDYING ENGLISH LITERATURE IN COLLEGE AND LIKES TO THINK OF HERSELF AS A SOUTHERN BELLE.

I love springtime. I love everything about it, especially the flowers. My favorite flower is a rose, but roses don't start blooming until early summer. Nothing is more maddening than watching all the other flowers bloom and having to wait several more weeks to see roses.

That's how I used to feel about waiting for my future husband. I thought it was a far-off event that would take forever to finally arrive. I felt as if I was missing out on a wonderful, exciting part of life. I saw my friends begin dating and my sister get married, and I felt cheated somehow.

SUSAN HORNER

I grew weary and frustrated and wanted to quit waiting and find someone—anyone—to fulfill the longing in my soul. Know what? I'm a twenty-year-old college student and I'm still waiting. But now, I'm actually enjoying it!

Instead of being frustrated by watching other flowers bloom while I wait for my rose, I can see the waiting process for its possibilities. I have some terrific guy friends who are incredibly fun to hang out with. We challenge and encourage each other to be all God created us to be.

God has a perfect plan for my life and will bring my husband along at just the right time—His time. The precious love I will share with my future husband will be worth all the years of waiting, hoping, hurting, and longing. I'm committed to waiting and saving myself because I know he will be like a rose—worth the wait.

When the hormonal alarm clock awakens your body, it switches on to autopilot. **You can't slow it down or speed it up.** You can help your body by exercising, eating healthy foods, drinking lots of water, and getting enough rest—but you cannot stop your feet from growing or make yourself grow taller.

This can be an exciting, pivotal time in your life. Honor yourself and God by making not just good, but great choices, and trusting God with your future. Whatever you do, do it all for the glory of God (1 Corinthians 10:31).

SUSAN HORNER

Ask God to help you discover your special talents!

Instead of focusing on what you cannot change about your developing body, focus on helping your mind, personality, and spirit grow. Read your Bible and talk to God. Ask Him to help you discover your special talents. Stretch yourself. Try something new. Maybe you'd like to try backpacking, rappelling off rocks with a certified instructor, running, lifting weights, or mountain biking. Or you might learn how to draw and paint. How about joining a team, like speech and debate, swimming, or tennis? **Have you ever wanted to try pottery, acting, fencing, snowshoeing,**

story writing, learning to play an instrument, or higher math or chess?

As you try new things you will discover your natural talents, although you may have to work hard and persevere before you have that feeling of accomplishment and skill. But you will be glad you did.

Choose friends who are kind, self-controlled, honest, and unselfish, then you will most likely marry someone who has these qualities as well. Learn how to share your thoughts by talking about books, movies, ideas, places you would like to visit, or favorite historical characters.

SUSAN HORNER

CHOOSE FRIENDS WHO ARE KIND, SELF-CONTROLLED, HONEST AND UNSELFISH!

Unless you take chances, you will never know what you are capable of doing. The choices you make today will affect how you feel tomorrow. Will you be happy and satisfied, or will you look back with regret?

This is the special season in your life. So go ahead—discover and develop your unique talents and gifts. Make great choices that will catapult you forward to reach your dreams and goals.

If you've been hurt . . .

God loves you, and you are precious in His sight.

A Gardener came upon a trampled garden and a stagnant, murky spring. The broken-down walls were easy to climb over, and the gate lay fallen on the ground. He wiped His eyes, thinking how the garden had been neglected and mistreated. He wanted the garden and spring for His own. It had cost Him something more valuable than silver or gold, but now they were His. First the Gardener rebuilt the walls. Then He made a new gate and hung it across the entrance. The Gardener cut the dead branches from the living trees. He pulled the tangled mess of choking weeds off the young plants and cleaned out the smelly, stagnant spring. The dry ground softened, and He planted roses and fragrant vines that had never grown there before.

SUSAN HORNER

*The garden came alive with new blossoms and fruit.
Then the Gardener stood back and said, "This garden would be
a beautiful place for a wedding." He looked down and
caught His reflection in the water and said, "And I would be there,
smiling upon the bride and groom."
John 15:1 says God the Father is a Gardener. Jesus took all of our bad
experiences from people sinning against us, and the sins that we choose to
do, upon Himself when He died on the cross. But Jesus did not stay dead.
He is alive and He wants to heal your broken heart, wash you as white as
snow, and place a crown upon your head. He hears you when you pray,
even if it is just a whisper.*

Since 1894, Moody Publishers has been dedicated to equip and motivate people to advance the cause of Christ by publishing evangelical Christian literature and other media for all ages, around the world. Because we are a ministry of the Moody Bible Institute of Chicago, a portion of the proceeds from the sale of this book go to train the next generation of Christian leaders.

If we may serve you in any way in your spiritual journey toward understanding Christ and the Christian life, please contact us at www.moodypublishers.com.

> *"All Scripture is God-breathed and is useful for teaching, rebuking, correcting and training in righteousness, so that the man of God may be thoroughly equipped for every good work."*
>
> —2 Timothy 3:16, 17

THE NAME YOU CAN TRUST®

More from Moody Publishers and Susan Horner

ISBN: 0-8024-0921-0

Why Do Plants Grow?

No one likes to wait, whether it's for dinner or to grow up. In *Why Do Plants Grow?* author and mother Susan Horner shows children how the life cycles of plants and seeds reflect God's amazing plan for all of His creation.

Why Do Birds Build Nests?

It's hard to mistake the cheerful call of a chickadee. In *Why Do Birds Build Nests?* author and mother Susan Horner explores how the lives of these songbirds illustrate God's wonderful plan for the reproduction of His creation.

ISBN: 0-8024-0922-9

ACQUIRING EDITOR:
Michele Straubel

COPY EDITOR:
Cheryl Dunlop

BACK COVER COPY:
Lisa Cockrel

COVER DESIGN:
LeVan Fisher Design

INTERIOR DESIGN:
Designs by Julia

PRINTING AND BINDING:
Color House Graphics

The typeface for the text of this book is
Baskerton